W9-BGM-328

A Guide for Using

The Chocolate Touch

in the Classroom

Based on the novel written by
Patrick Skene Catling

This guide written by **Lorraine Kujawa**

Teacher Created Resources, Inc.
6421 Industry Way
Westminster, CA 92683
www.teachercreated.com
ISBN: 978-1-57690-337-7
©*1999 Teacher Created Resources, Inc.*
Reprinted, 2011
Made in U.S.A.

Edited by
Mary Lou Hjort

Illustrated by
Wendy Chang

Cover Art by
Wendy Chang

Table of Contents

Introduction

A good book can become a good friend. It can cause us to be informed, to imagine, and to be inspired in the days to come. You never feel alone with a good book. Each time we read a good book, we become reacquainted and learn something new. Each new story will last a lifetime.

In Literature Units, we take great care to select books that will become close friends.

Teachers using this unit will enjoy the following features that will add to their own valuable ideas:

- Sample Lesson Plan

- Pre-reading Activities

- A Biographical Sketch of the Author

- A Book Summary

- Vocabulary Lists and Vocabulary Activity Ideas

- Chapters grouped for study with sections that include the following:

    —*quizzes*

    —*hands-on projects*

    —*cooperative learning activities*

    —*cross-curriculum connections*

    —*extensions into the reader's own life*

- Post-reading Activities

- Book Report Ideas

- A Culminating Activity

- Research Ideas

- Three Different Options for a Unit Test

- Bibliography of Related Reading

- Answer Key

We are confident that using this unit will have a positive impact upon your planning, and your students will learn to cherish the stories you present to them.

Sample Lesson Plan

Each of the lessons below can take one or several days to complete, depending on your schedule.

Lesson 1
- Introduce and complete some or all of the pre-reading activities (pages 5 and 6).
- Initiate the Reader's Guide (page 7).
- Read About the Author with your students (page 8). Discuss the questions at the bottom of the page.
- Read the Book Summary with your students (page 9).
- Introduce Section 1 of the vocabulary (page 10).

Lesson 2
- Read chapters 1 through 3. As you read each chapter, take notes in your Reader's Guide.
- Discuss the vocabulary as it appears in the book.
- Do a vocabulary activity (page 11).
- Have students follow the directions for making a Magic Chocolate Box (page 13).
- Discuss what is in the chocolate that people eat (page 15).
- Follow directions for the Banana Pudding Tart (page 16).
- Discuss the difference between Needs and Wants (page 17).
- Give Section 1 quiz (page 12).
- Introduce Section 2 vocabulary (page 10).

Lesson 3
- Read chapters 4 through 6. Record notes in the Reader's Guide.
- Discuss the vocabulary as it appears in the book.
- Do a vocabulary activity (page 11).
- Work on an art project (page 19).
- Write a Chocolate Rap (page 20).

- Work with synonyms (page 21).
- Write letters to candy companies (pages 22–23).
- Give Section 2 quiz (page 18).
- Introduce Section 3 vocabulary (page 10).

Lesson 4
- Read chapters 7 through 9. Do a vocabulary activity (page 11).
- Organize the Apple Dunking activity (page 25).
- Organize groups for the Eating Well activity (pages 26–27).
- Read the information sheet and answer questions on how chocolate is made (pages 28–29).
- Consider how much chocolate you consume (page 30).
- Give Section 3 quiz (page 24).
- Introduce Section 4 vocabulary (page 10).

Lesson 5
- Read chapters 10 through 12.
- Discuss the vocabulary words in context.
- Introduce a vocabulary activity (page 11).
- Create a Homemade Elixir (page 32).
- Write stories in small groups (page 33).
- Make a map of your school (pages 34–35).
- Survey people's needs (page 36).
- Give Section 4 quiz (page 31).

Lesson 6
- Discuss any questions the students may have about the story.
- Do a research project on chocolate (page 40).

Before the Book

Tales or stories like *The Chocolate Touch* teach a lesson in a way that makes what the author wants to say easier to understand. Patrick Skene Catling tells the story of a young boy who wanted chocolate so much that he was not concerned with anything else. The ancient Greeks also told a story about a person who wanted something so much that he forgot what was important in his life. It is called *The Midas Touch*. Read this Greek story and think of the lesson it might tell.

The Midas Touch

Once upon a time in the land of Greece by the Aegean Sea there was a great king named Midas. King Midas was a good man in his heart, but he had one weakness. He yearned for gold. He would spend all his time counting his gold coins and wishing for more. He had a lovely garden, but he did not spend time there. He had two wonderful hounds who loved to run in the fields, but he did not take the time to be with them. He had a beautiful daughter named Marigold whom he truly loved, yet he did not spend time with her. He spent all his time counting his gold coins in the basement vault of the castle.

One evening when it was very late and all the servants were asleep, the hounds were resting before the fire, the flowers had closed their petals for the night, and the king's daughter was quietly tucked away in her sleeping chamber, King Midas was alone in the vault in the basement, counting his many bags of gold and wondering just how many coins were in each bag. Out of nowhere the form of a stranger appeared to King Midas.

The stranger said, "King Midas, you have much gold!"

King Midas was startled but replied, "It is much, but nothing compared to all the gold in the world."

"Are you not satisfied?" the stranger said to the King.

"Oh, no. I am always trying to find ways to gather more gold. I wish that everything I touched would turn to gold."

"Are you sure you would want that?" asked the stranger.

The King replied, "I could think of nothing that would make me happier."

"You may have your wish," the stranger said and disappeared.

The King was so excited! He touched the doorknob of the vault and found that it had turned to gold.

"How wonderful, how marvelous!" he exclaimed.

He could now have all the gold he wanted. As the sun rose, the King ordered his servants to prepare a feast to celebrate his new gift. However, when he sat down to the feast and reached for a piece of bread, it turned to gold. He was shocked. The King lifted a mug of water to his lips, and it, too, became gold. This upset the King so that he rose from his seat and went out into the garden. His two hounds followed him.

Before the Book (cont.)

While he was walking and thinking, the King reached out to smell a flower. It, too, turned to gold. He drew back. When he did, he touched the heads of his two hounds. Instantly, they both turned to graceful statues of gold. King Midas cried out in distress. Just then his daughter, who had heard him cry out, ran to him.

"Father, Father, what has happened that you would cry out?"

Before he could stop her, Marigold threw her arms around her father to hug him. She immediately turned to gold!

"What have I done!" cried the King. He wept loudly as he realized how his foolish wish had caused the loss of his daughter. As he was weeping, the stranger appeared again to King Midas.

"Are you not happy now that you have the golden touch? Why do you cry out?"

"I have lost all that I have loved. Give me back my daughter, and I will give up all the gold that I have in my entire kingdom!"

"You are a wiser man," said the stranger. "Do as I say, and you will lose the golden touch. Follow the river that runs through your kingdom to where it flows from the mountain. Walk into the river so that you become completely immersed in water. You will then lose your golden touch. Take a pitcher of water back with you to the palace and sprinkle the water on all that you have touched, and it will be changed back."

The King did as he was told. He followed the river to the mountain. He immersed himself in the river. He touched the rocks in the river and realized that he no longer had the golden touch. He rushed back to the castle with a pitcher of water and sprinkled his daughter with it. She came back to life immediately, and he hugged her with happiness. Then the King sprinkled his hounds with water, and they were no longer statues but jumping, running hounds. The King then sprinkled the flowers in the garden and bent to smell each one as they became real again. He was so happy that he lifted his daughter, Marigold, to dance about the garden with him.

After that day, King Midas was a wise and generous king and would always warn people, "Be careful what you wish for. You might get your wish."

The end.

Before you read *The Chocolate Touch*, do one of these activities so you may understand what John is going through in the story.

1. There are many ways people can become greedy for one or many things. Discuss, in groups of three, what people can want too much of. Discuss how wanting too much of something can become a problem. What can happen if you want too many friends? too many shoes? too much money? Have one person in the group be the scribe and write down an example of one thing that can cause a problem and what that problem may be if you were to want too much of it. Share your ideas with the class.

2. Draw two pictures. Draw the first picture about what you might want too much of. The second picture could be of what might happen if you actually got your wish. Share your work with the class and tell what might have gone wrong.

3. Discuss with the students in your class what might happen to the boy in the book, John Midas, who wanted chocolate all the time.

Reader's Guide

Having a guide to a book you read helps you understand how the story unfolds. It is also enjoyable to have a collection of activities when the book is complete. Here are some suggestions of how to assemble your guide.

1. **The cover:** You will need two sheets of 8 $\frac{1}{2}$" x 11" (22 cm x 28 cm) of stiff paper. Neatly print the title of the book, *The Chocolate Touch*, the author's name, and your name on the cover. Decorate the cover with pictures of chocolate or paste labels from chocolate products on the cover. Be careful to leave space for the book title and names. If it is possible, have the cover and back laminated so it will hold up.

2. **The interior:** You will need 14 sheets of lined paper and 7 sheets of unlined paper. Number your lined paper with page numbers 1, 4, 6, 7, 8, 10, 11, 12, 13, 15, 17, 18, 20, and t.c. for the table of contents. Number your unlined papers with page numbers 2, 3, 5, 9, 14, 16, and 19. Put them in order and connect the covers and the papers with paper fasteners or a stapler.

3. **The table of contents:** Include the following information in your table of contents.

Vocabulary words and sentences from chapters 1–3. 1

Drawings and written descriptions of main characters 2

Chocolate candy wrapper collection 3

Writing about what happened in chapters 1, 2, and 3: setting, mood,
    problem that arose, and prediction of what will happen 4

Drawings of what happened in each chapter (1–3) 5

List of your five needs and your five wants 6

Vocabulary words and sentences from chapters 4–6 7

Writing about what happened in chapters 4, 5, and 6: setting, mood,
    problem that arose, and prediction of what will happen 8

Drawings of what happened in each chapter (4–6) 9

Chocolate Rap 10

List of companies you could write to for information 11

Vocabulary words and sentences from chapters 7–9 12

Writing about what happened in chapters 7, 8, and 9: setting, mood,
    problem that arose, and prediction of what will happen 13

Drawings of what happened in each chapter (7–9) 14

Menu of a balanced diet for one day 15

Colorful drawing of how chocolate is made 16

Vocabulary words and sentences from chapters 10–12 17

Writing about what happened in chapters 10, 11, and 12: setting, mood,
    problem that arose, and how it was solved 18

Drawings of what happened in each chapter (10–12) 19

Paragraph of what you enjoyed most about *The Chocolate Touch* 20

About the Author

Patrick Skene Catling was born in London, England, on February 14, 1925. He flew planes in the earlier part of his life for the Royal Canadian Air Force. Catling writes for adults as well as children. He is also an essayist, expressing in magazines his opinions about many topics in the world.

Catling immigrated to the United States in 1956 and became a citizen of the U.S. He worked as a magazine editor for the *Baltimore Sun*, the *Manchester Guardian*, *Punch*, and *Newsweek*. He became a freelance writer (a person who gets paid for stories he chooses to write) in 1964.

In 1952 Catling wrote *The Chocolate Touch*. He received the Utah Children's Book Award for this book.

Catling has written more than ten books for adults in his lifetime. Some of them are science fiction, like *The Exterminator*, which is about a man who becomes a rat. Some are light fantasies, and some are realistic.

Catling's latest children's book, *John Midas in the Dreamtime*, is the story of a boy who visits the site of the sacred paintings in the Australian Outback and is transported thousands of years back in time to find himself among a prehistoric aboriginal tribe.

Questions for Young Writers

After reading about Patrick Skene Catling, respond to these questions. Share your ideas with the class.

- What kind of experiences would an author have to have to write about some of the unusual things that Catling has written about?

  _____

  _____

- Why is it important to write about what you know and have experienced?

  _____

  _____

- What could Catling have experienced that would help him write a book like *The Chocolate Touch*?

  _____

  _____

The Chocolate Touch

by Patrick Skene Catling

(William Morrow and Company, Inc., 1952 and 1979)

(Available in Canada, Gage Distributors; UK, International Book Distributors; AUS, Kirby Book Company)

The Chocolate Touch is a story about a boy named John Midas who had an unusual desire for chocolate. His desire for chocolate got him into serious trouble.

John, usually a nice boy, lived with his younger sister Mary, his gentle mother, and his understanding father who told him interesting things about beetles and birds' nests. He liked school but loved candy, mostly chocolate.

John's parents thought John was eating too much candy. They took him to see Dr. Cranium who gave John a tonic to keep him healthy.

One Sunday afternoon John found a strange coin with the initials J. M. on one side. He also found an unusual candy store where he traded his coin for a box of chocolates. When John undid the box and its trimmings, he found that there was only one piece of chocolate in the entire box. He was disappointed but immediately ate the single chocolate. It was an extraordinary piece of chocolate.

The next morning, John was delighted to find that everything that touched his mouth became chocolate! This gift turned to disaster when John bit Susan Buttercup's birthday silver dollar and came away with a bite of chocolate, and she was left with a crescent of a coin. Panic followed as John turned his pencil into solid chocolate, turned water from the school water fountain into liquid chocolate, and even his trumpet became a sticky statue of chocolate.

John's panic escalated when he dunked for apples at Susan Buttercup's birthday party and turned the bucket of water into syrupy chocolate liquid and ruined her dress. John ran home in disgrace.

John's father helped John look for the candy shop where all John's problems began. All they found was an empty lot with a "For Sale" sign on it.

John's father returned John to Dr. Cranium's office. After John changed the doctor's spoon and elixir into chocolate, Dr. Cranium declared that John was a victim of Chocolitis or Cranium's Disease. When they returned home and told John's mother that John had Cranium's Disease, she began to cry. Without thinking, John kissed his mother's cheek and turned her to chocolate!

John became frantic and ran from the house to find the candy shop. He found it this time and blamed the storekeeper for his problems. The storekeeper made him realize that it was John's responsibility all along. John pleaded to have his mother returned to normal. John would have to make the choice to give up the chocolate touch in order to restore his mother. His choice was to help his mother.

When John arrived home, his mother had been returned to normal. John no longer had the chocolate touch, and everything was the way it had been.

John returned to the lot where the candy store had been to thank the storekeeper, but he found only an empty lot with a sign that said, "Sold."

Vocabulary Lists

On this page are the vocabulary lists which correspond to each sectional grouping of chapters. Vocabulary activities can be found on page 11 of this book.

Section 1 *(Chapters 1–3)*

pretending	lozenges	complications	tonic	bristles
suitable	nougat	gleaming	cotton batting	tilted
practical	marrons glacés	initials	revealing	protested
toffee	cranium	beckoning	marvelous	marmalade

Section 2 *(Chapters 4–6)*

devouring	triumphs	scuffling	signal	scorned
slyest	suspiciously	spectacles	corridor	sacrifice
snatched	reluctantly	swiftly	enamel	glee
gutter	crescent	accurately	reproachfully	retorted

Section 3 *(Chapters 7–9)*

securely	persuade	absent	echoed	desperately
spacious	morsel	auditorium	baton	halted
quenching	opaque	confidence	solo	drenched
appetizing	avarice	promptly	flustered	delicate

Section 4 *(Chapters 10–12)*

dreadful	elixir	lace	satisfaction	selfishness
stroll	brimful	abruptly	interrupted	frantically
fantasy	spurted	rubbish	evident	crockery
peered	exhaustive	proprietor	acquiring	briskly

Vocabulary Activity Ideas

You can help your students learn and retain the vocabulary in *The Chocolate Touch* by providing them with interesting vocabulary activities. Here are some ideas to try.

❑ **Alphabetizing Contest**—Each group of three students gets a resealable plastic bag of vocabulary cards. Have floor space for each group. When the teacher says, "Go," dump the cards out and put the words in alphabetical order. When the students are done, they stand up and say, "Done!" Give prizes for the first correct list.

❑ **Shout Down!**—Each student in a group of three gets a card with one vocabulary word on it. Each looks up his or her word in the dictionary and writes down a sentence using the word correctly. The student comes to the teacher's desk to have the sentence checked. After the "OK" from the teacher, the student returns to his or her group to practice saying the sentence. When all are done, call on each group to *shout* their sentences, emphasizing their vocabulary words.

❑ **Vocabulary Cube**—Each student cuts out six 4" (12 cm) squares from poster board. Write a different vocabulary word on three of the squares. Write the definitions of the words on the other three squares. Tape the edges together to form a cube.

❑ **Toss and Say**—Using the vocabulary cubes that the students made in the previously listed activity, toss a cube to a student. Whatever word or meaning lands on the top, the student must give the meaning or the word for it. Points will be given to teams that give correct answers.

❑ **Coupon Cards**—Give students cards on their desks in the morning with a vocabulary word on each. The card can be exchanged like a coupon during the day for chocolate candy by using the word in a sentence correctly to the teacher.

❑ **Picture Dictionary**—Cut 11 sheets of 8 ½" x 11" (22 cm x 28 cm) paper in half. Staple at one side. Label the cover My Picture Dictionary, Volume 1. On each page at the top, write a vocabulary word and the definition. At the bottom, write one sentence using the word. In the center, create and color a picture demonstrating the sentence. Use a few words each day from the list to practice building your vocabulary.

❑ **Word Chain**—Each student cuts strips of paper 1" x 6" (2.54 cm x 15 cm). Write a vocabulary word on each one, leaving about ½" (1 cm) at either end for pasting. Loop the strips through each other and paste the ends together to form a chain. The student puts the chain around his or her neck when finished and refers to the words during the day.

❑ **Vocabulary Floor Team Game**—Make a chart of the vocabulary words in 5" (13 cm) squares. Have the chart laminated if possible. Each student stands about 3' (1 m) away and tosses a an aluminum foil ball onto the chart. Whatever word it lands on must be used correctly in a sentence.

❑ **Vocabulary Shapes**—Have the students select several vocabulary words from each chapter. Ask them to lightly draw shapes (in pencil) that remind them of the words. Next, tell them to write the words around the edges of the shapes as many times as they can in marker, crayon, or colored pencil. This is an excellent activity for the students to do in their free time. It also makes a creative and attractive bulletin board.

Quiz Time!

Answer the following questions about chapters 1, 2, and 3 in sentences. You may use your book.

1. Is the first line of chapter 1 more or less interesting than the first line of chapter 2? Why do you think so?

   _____

2. Name the types of candy John loves.

   _____

   _____

   _____

   _____

3. Why does John refuse the extra money his mother offers him to buy chocolates?

   _____

4. Who is named Cranium in the story? Why is this a good name for the person?

   _____

5. Are John's parents kind? Give three reasons why you feel this is true.

   _____

   _____

   _____

6. Why does John hide the box under the bed at home?

   _____

7. What is unusual about the coin that John found?

   _____

8. What is the first clue that something is going wrong?

   _____

9. What is in the box John brings home from the candy store?

   _____

10. Do you think John will get into trouble? Have you ever gotten into trouble because you made the wrong decision? Explain.

   _____

   _____

   _____

Magic Chocolate Box

At the end of chapter 2 of *The Chocolate Touch,* John had purchased what he thought was a whole box of chocolate candy. What a surprise when he found only one chocolate in the box!

There were six things that John came across before he got to the chocolate. List in order what John found before he unwrapped the chocolate candy:

1. _____

2. _____

3. _____

4. _____

5. _____

6. _____

7. chocolate candy in foil

Collect the items you will need for putting your Magic Chocolate Box together. They are listed below:

- scissors
- cardboard
- shredded paper
- box pattern as shown on page 14
- chocolate kiss or other wrapped chocolate candy
- glue or tape
- silver or gold foil
- cotton batting
- sheet of cellophane

Follow the directions on page 14 to assemble the box. (**Note:** For durability, reproduce the pattern on index or other heavy paper.) Place the items for your box in the exact opposite order of your list, starting with the wrapped chocolate. Go backwards on your list until your box is set up exactly the way John found his Magic Chocolate Box.

When your Magic Chocolate Box is neatly wrapped in the cellophane, take it home to give to someone. Do not tell them what is in it and watch their surprise when they find the magic chocolate inside.

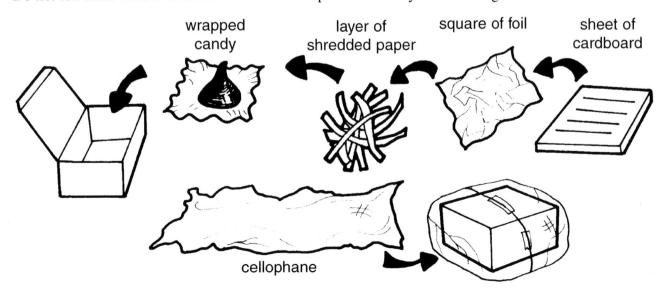

wrapped candy   layer of shredded paper   square of foil   sheet of cardboard

cellophane

Magic Chocolate Box *(cont.)*

Directions

1. Cut the pattern along the solid lines.

2. Fold the box down along the dashed lines.

3. Glue the tabs to the box edges, matching the letters.

Note: Do not tape the lid tab until the items have been placed in the box.

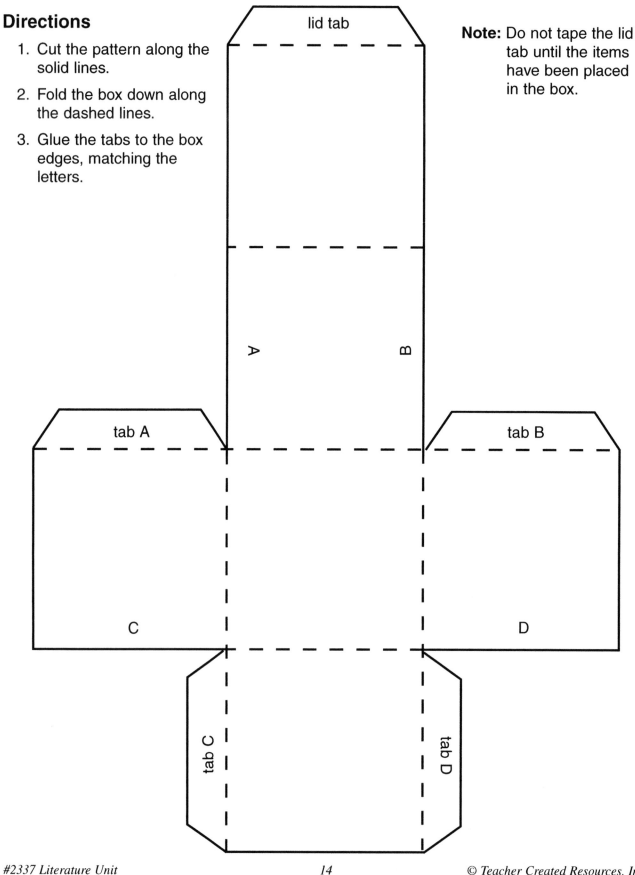

What's in Chocolate Candy?

John has a problem with eating too much of one kind of food. His mother feels that it is not healthy to eat only one thing. If John had read the labels on the candy bars that he ate, he would have known what he was eating.

Below is a sample candy wrapper. There are many other ingredients in a chocolate bar besides chocolate. The candy bar below has seven ingredients. The most of what a product has in it is always listed first. The ingredient that represents the least amount is listed last.

CHOCOLATE GOODY ALMOND BAR

INGREDIENTS: MILK CHOCOLATE (MILK CHOCOLATE CONTAINS SUGAR; MILK; COCOA BUTTER; CHOCOLATE; SOYA LECITHIN, AN EMULSIFIER; AND VANILLIN, AN ARTIFICIAL FLAVORING); AND ALMONDS

	Amt. per serving	%DV		Amt. per serving	%DV
Total Fat	14g	22%	**Total Carbohydrates**	20g	7%
Saturated Fat	7g	35%	Dietary Fiber	1g	5%
Cholesterol	.5mg	2%	Sugars	18g	
Sodium	35mg	30%	**Protein**	5g	
Vitamin A 0% Vitamin C 0% Calcium 8% Iron 4%					

Nutrition Facts

Serving Size 1 Bar

Calories 220

Fat Cal. 120

Percent Daily Values (DV) are based on a 2,000 calorie diet.

Check this label carefully and list the milk chocolate contents of this candy bar from the greatest amount to the least amount.

1. _____   5. _____
2. _____   6. _____
3. _____   7. _____
4. _____

Now that you are acquainted with how to read labels, you will have a chance to check out the ingredients of other chocolate candies. With a partner, take some time to collect five different chocolate bar labels. Copy the form below for a total of five copies and complete a form for each candy bar. Take turns looking up ingredients that you do not understand.

- -

Name of chocolate candy: _____

Ingredients: _____

_____

Difficult word and definition: _____

_____

Banana Pudding Tart

Not only does John Midas enjoy chocolate in candy bars, he enjoys chocolate in other foods. Something that John might have enjoyed doing on a Saturday afternoon might be following the directions of a recipe to make something with a chocolate taste. The following is a recipe for Banana Pudding Tart. A tart is a small shallow pie without a top crust, filled with fruit or custard. Tarts are very popular in France.

In order to make this tart, you will need to gather these ingredients and utensils:

- 2 bananas
- 2 boxes of instant chocolate pudding
- 2 cups (500 mL) of milk for the pudding
- 1 box of graham crackers
- 1 shallow pan, about 9" (23 cm) square
- 1 large spoon for stirring and layering the pudding

- 1 bowl for mixing the pudding
- measuring cup for milk
- 1 knife for cutting
- several bowls and spoons for serving and eating the tart
- paper towels for cleaning up

Follow the directions on the box to mix the instant pudding. Once done, put the rest of the ingredients together as follows: Break up graham crackers to line the bottom of the pan. Spread $\frac{1}{3}$ layer of pudding over the crackers. Slice bananas so that they form small circles. Place the slices in a layer over the pudding. Spread broken graham crackers across the top of the bananas. Layer again with chocolate pudding. Continue layering with graham crackers, bananas, and pudding until you have three layers. Place the tart in the refrigerator until chilled (about one hour). Clean up your working space and your utensils. When the tart is chilled, spoon portions of it into individual serving bowls or plates and eat.

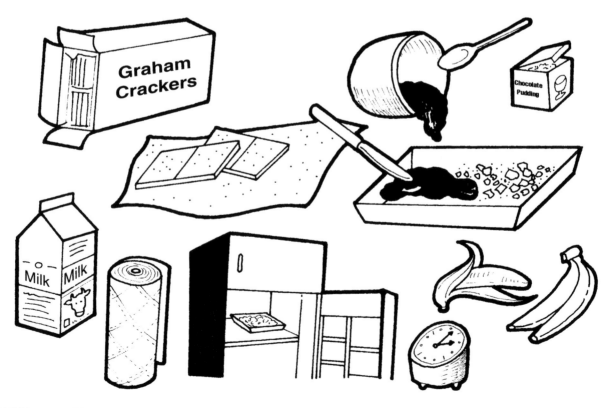

Needs and Wants

In *The Chocolate Touch*, John Midas is called greedy by the storekeeper. Do you think John is greedy? People often get confused by their needs and their wants. Here are the definitions of each.

- **greed (grēd)**—*n.* **an excessive desire to acquire or possess more than what one needs or deserves**
- **need (nēd)**—*n.* **something required**
- **want (wŏnt)**—*n.* **to desire greatly, wish for**

See if you can tell the difference between real needs and ordinary wants. List 10 things that you would like to have and check the appropriate box to indicate whether you think it is a want or need. Discuss with an adult which ones are things you really need and which ones are things you want.

What You Wish For	Want	Need
1.		
2.		
3.		
4.		
5.		
6.		
7.		
8.		
9.		
10.		

Quiz Time!

Answer the following questions about chapters 4, 5, and 6 in sentences. You may use your book to find the answers.

1. What changes for John when he gets up in the morning?

_____

_____

2. Why does Spider Wilson say that John has gone crazy?

_____

3. Why does Susan say that she hates John?

_____

4. What is beginning to go wrong for John?

_____

_____

5. Why does John look in dismay at the puddle of water in the water fountain?

_____

6. What change is happening to John in chapter 5?

_____

_____

7. What do you think people will say if John tells them about the magic?

_____

_____

8. List three unexpected things that have happened so far in these three chapters.

_____

_____

_____

9. List four rules that you think John should follow.

_____

_____

_____

_____

10. What lesson do you think John is learning from his experience with chocolate?

_____

Character Poster

The characters in *The Chocolate Touch* are all very interesting. It can be fun to depict each of the characters in a picture form. Some of them are adults, like John's mother, and some are your age, like the boy who tried to eat John's glove. Below is a list of the characters. Choose one with your partner and collect the materials needed for this project.

Characters

John Midas	Mr. Midas	Dr. Cranium	Spider Wilson
Mrs. Midas	Mary Midas	Susan Buttercup	Storekeeper

Materials

- butcher paper (enough for the length of each student's body)
- paints
- markers

- pencil
- masking tape
- several sheets of white paper
- ruler

Directions

1. With your partner, trace your body on a large sheet of butcher paper. It helps to tape the ends of the paper to the floor. Do not tape the corners as the paper will tear when you lift it up. Draw in the features of the character you have chosen. Paint on the clothing of the character. Use your book if you need to refresh your memory.

2. Using a ruler, draw two guidelines 2" (5 cm) apart in the upper right-hand corner of the butcher paper with your pencil. Use markers to carefully print the name of the character between the guidelines.

3. Use a ruler, to draw guidelines on a white sheet of paper. Use the guidelines for printing. In large letters, write what the person you drew was like. Draw guidelines, using a ruler, on another sheet of paper and tell what part the character played in the story. Use a third sheet to tell the name of the book and the author's name.

4. Paste the three sheets neatly on your butcher paper, being careful not to cover any of your painting.

5. Place your name at the bottom of your artwork or on the back of the poster.

6. Hang all the posters in the hall for other students to see.

The Chocolate Rap

Imagine that John loved chocolate so much he made up the following rap (song) about the qualities of chocolate.

I love chocolate
Rich and creamy,
Even in pudding
Smooth and steamy.

Eat it in hunks.
Eat it on chips.
Eat it in bars.
Taste it in dips.

Chocolate on potatoes,
Chocolate on peas,
Chocolate in the pool,
Up to your knees.

I love chocolate
Any way you make it.
Just give me chocolate,
And I'll take it.

Create Your Own Rap

John may have changed his mind about chocolate after he got his wish to have as much as he wanted and more.

1. With a partner, make up a chocolate rap that tells how John loves chocolate and gets into trouble because of it. The rap should have at least 16 lines to tell the whole story.

2. Write the rap, placing each phrase on a separate line as in the poem above.

3. Practice the rap with your partner until you both know it well. You can snap your fingers to the beat or put small pebbles in a box and shake it to the beat. (Make sure that the box is securely taped so the pebbles don't fall out.)

4. Present your rap to the class. Keep the words so you can present your rap at the Chocolate Party when you have finished reading the book.

In Other Words

To make a story more interesting, a writer might replace a frequently used word or phrase with an appropriate phrase or synonym (a word that means the same or almost the same as another) that expresses the same idea but in other words. For example, in *The Chocolate Touch,* the author replaces the words "warmer than usual" with "temperature" in the following sentences:

> "She placed her hand on John's forehead to feel whether he was warmer than usual. 'But I don't think he has a temperature,' she decided."

Below is a puzzle that fits together to form a picture of a famous candy. Cut the pieces apart and match up the words that are synonyms. If you need to use your word list or the dictionary, do so.

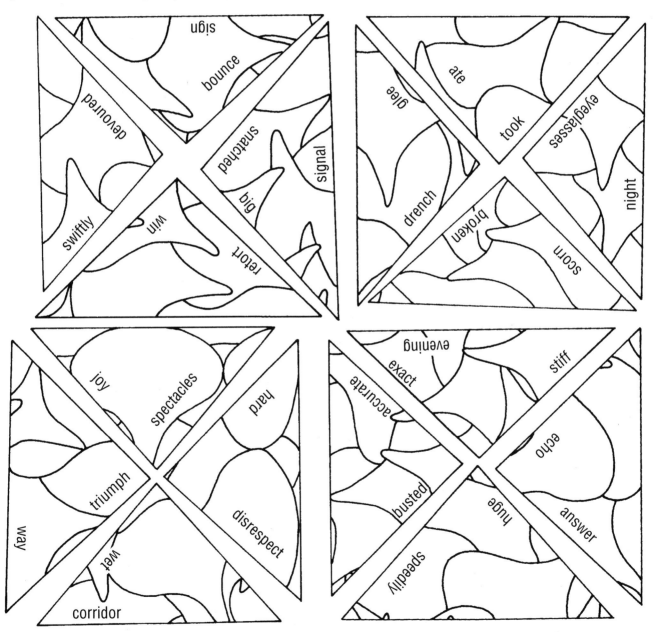

After assembling your puzzle, use five of your words and their synonyms in a sentence, using the same sentence for each pair of synonyms. Example: The sidewalk was hot. The sidewalk was sizzling.

Letters to the Companies

Most people love candy. Perhaps most people don't love candy as much as John Midas did, but candy is a favorite thing to eat.

In *The Chocolate Touch*, the author lists all of John's favorite treats.

> "He was a pig about candy. Boiled candy, licorice all-sorts, old-fashioned toffee, candied orange and lemon slices, crackerjack, jellybeans, fudge, black-currant lozenges for ticklish throats, nougat, marrons glacés, acid crops, peppermint sticks, lollipops, marshmallows, and above all, chocolates—he devoured them all."

It is exciting to taste all those wonderful treats, but it is also interesting to know how they are made. You could get information about these treats by writing to the companies that manufacture them.

Imagine that you have a suggestion for a new candy. Prepare a business letter as though you were explaining your new idea to a candy company. Just pretend you are sending the letter.

Before you write your letter there are some rules you need to follow so you can be sure the information gets there.

How to Write a Business Letter

Materials

- writing paper
- pen
- envelope
- stamp
- address of company

Writing the Business Letter

1. The company will need to know your address so they can send you an answer. **Place your address in the upper right-hand corner of the writing paper. Place the date under your address** so they will know when it was sent to them. This section is called the **return address**.

2. Some companies have many offices in the same building, so you need to make sure your letter will get to the correct office. **Put their address on the left side of your writing paper under your address.** This is called the **inside address**.

3. **Place Dear Candy Company:** (or whatever the name of the candy company is) **on the left side under the inside address.** This is called the **greeting**.

4. Now write what you have to say. **Begin the letter two spaces beneath the greeting. You do not have to indent in a business letter.** Begin by mentioning something about their product that you enjoy. Skip a line to begin the second paragraph to tell them about your idea for a new kind of candy. Skip a line for the last paragraph. Thank them for their time and consideration of your idea. All of this is called the **body** of the letter.

Letters to the Companies *(cont.)*

5. Of course, you will need to sign your entire name, first and last, so the mail carrier will be able to give you rather than your neighbor the mail the company might send to you. **Skip a line and write Sincerely, and sign your full name neatly under it**. This is called the **closing** and the **signature**.

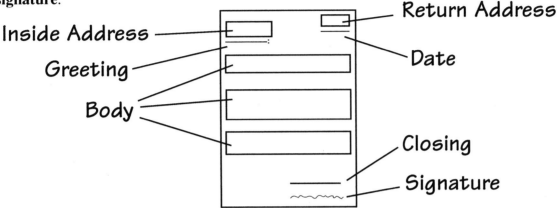

Preparing the Envelope

1. You need an envelope and a stamp. **Use a business envelope which is 4 $\frac{1}{8}$" x 9 $\frac{1}{2}$"** **(11 cm x 24 cm)**. The stamp goes in the upper right-hand corner of the front of the envelope. Without it, the letter would go nowhere. **Just draw a stamp since we are pretending to send this one**.

2. You need to put the **company's address in the center of the front of the envelope**. Make sure you include the zip code. Print or write neatly, or the letter will not get to its destination.

3. In case the company you write to has moved or closed down or the stamp falls off, the post office would like to give you your letter back. So you need to have a **return address**. **Write or print clearly, your name and address in the top left-hand corner of the front of the envelope**. It should be smaller than the company's address. Some people have address labels that they use instead of writing their addresses out.

4. Fold the letter in thirds from the bottom up and then from the top down. Slip it into the envelope.

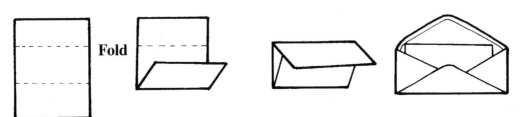

Quiz Time!

Answer the following questions about chapters 7, 8, and 9 in sentences. You may use your book to find the answers.

1. Why does John envy a boy in the lunchroom? _____

   _____

2. What has John's major fear become? _____

   _____

3. What new trick does John try? _____

   _____

4. What new events are beginning to happen to John? _____

   _____

5. What instrument does John play in the orchestra? _____

   _____

   What happens to it? _____

   _____

6. Why do you think John is so angry at Miss Plimsole, Mrs. Quaver, the school, and Susan?

   _____

   _____

7. What does John say to make his mother worry about him? _____

   _____

   _____

8. What makes you think that Susan likes John? _____

   _____

   _____

9. What is the final game at the party? _____

   _____

10. If someone says, "It went from bad to worse," how would that apply to John?_____

   _____

   _____

   _____

Apple Dunking

When the Buttercup family planned Susan's party, they included ducking for apples. *The Chocolate Touch* is a book that was written in England. Though the British people in England do speak English, many of their words are different from ours. Ducking is one of them. *Dunking* means to plunge into a liquid. When John and Susan *ducked* for apples, they plunged into the water for the apples, or *dunked.*

Do you know of any other English words from England that are different from our American English? Here are some words from England you may enjoy knowing:

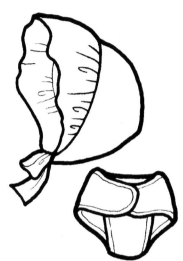

boot—trunk of a car

bonnet—hood of a car

nappies—diapers

ring up—to call on the telephone

petrol—gasoline

lay-by—a pull-over spot on the road

scones—muffins

underground—subway

holiday—vacation

pram—baby carriage

Ducking and dunking for apples can be an enjoyable experience.

Materials

- enough apples for all the participants
- a wide bucket with room enough for two people to dunk at a time
- towels to dry people's faces and hair
- If you dunk inside, you will need newspaper on the floor under and around the bucket to catch the water. Wipe up the spills before they become too messy.
- water

Directions

- Place the tub in the center of the room with the papers under it.
- Fill the tub halfway with water.
- Divide the class into two teams or just take turns dunking.
- Kneel at the tub with your hands behind your back. Dunk your head in the water to retrieve the apple with your teeth. To catch an apple on the first try, you need to be bold.

Note to teacher: You may wish to skip this activity of actually dunking for apples due to hygiene concerns or get permission to have students participate.

Eating Well

Nutrition is an important part of caring for yourself. John Midas's mother was very concerned about what John ate.

The Food Pyramid was created by the United States Department of Agriculture (USDA) as a way of presenting the latest guidelines for a healthful diet. The following pyramid shows what a daily balanced diet looks like. Use the chart information to create a menu that reflects what you think are healthful foods to eat each day. Use the form on page 27 to write your menu. Share your daily diet ideas with the class.

The Food Pyramid

A Guide to Daily Food Choices

Key
● Fat (naturally occurring and added)
▼ Sugars (added)

These symbols show that fat and added sugars come mostly from fats, oils, and sweets but can be part of or added to foods from the food groups as well.

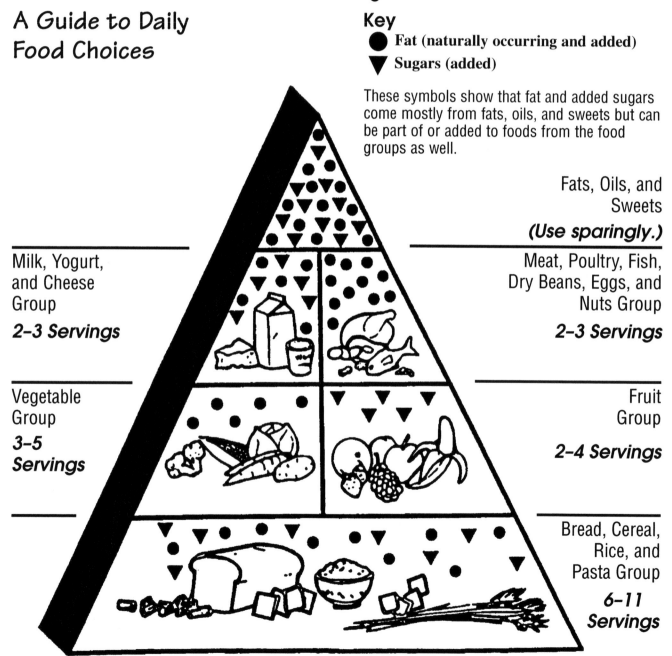

Fats, Oils, and Sweets
(Use sparingly.)

Milk, Yogurt, and Cheese Group
2–3 Servings

Meat, Poultry, Fish, Dry Beans, Eggs, and Nuts Group
2–3 Servings

Vegetable Group
3–5 Servings

Fruit Group
2–4 Servings

Bread, Cereal, Rice, and Pasta Group
6–11 Servings

Eating Well *(cont.)*

Sunshine Restaurant

Owner:_____

Breakfast

_____

_____

_____

_____

_____

_____

Lunch

_____

_____

_____

_____

_____

_____

Dinner

_____

_____

_____

_____

_____

_____

_____

_____

_____

Snacks (Desserts, Appetizers)

_____

_____

_____

_____

How Chocolate Is Made

The storekeeper told John Midas that some of his chocolate came from Africa. Here are some facts you may not know about chocolate. Use them to answer the questions on page 29.

- Chocolate is grown in many parts of the world but mostly in tropical areas like Mexico, Central America, South America, and Africa.

- Brazil is the largest producer of cacao beans in the Western Hemisphere.

- Cacao is the common name that comes from the Mayan Indian words that mean *bitter juice*.

- The word chocolate comes from the Mayan words that mean *sour water*.

- A cacao tree can reach a height of 40 feet (12 meters).

- The leaves of the cacao tree are elliptical and up to a foot long.

- Flowers on the cacao tree are small, wax-like, yellow, and grow directly on the trunk and branches of the tree. The flowers turn into *pods* 8 to 15 inches (20–38 cm) long, the size of a large cucumber. Inside the pods are 20 to 50 almond-shaped seeds or beans in a shell. The beans are removed by hand, using a large knife to cut open the pod. They are commonly called *cocoa beans*.

- The beans are put in a sweatbox for nine days to ferment. After they have fermented, the cocoa beans are set to dry in the sun, then put in bags and sent to the manufacturer.

- The manufacturer combines a special mixture of different types of cocoa beans for a variety of products.

- The beans are cleaned and then roasted so that their shells expand.

- An unusual machine with a fan blows the shells off the beans.

- The shells are used for mulch and fertilizer. You can purchase them at your local plant store. They give off the lovely scent of chocolate in your garden if used as mulch.

- The meat of the bean that is left is called the *nibs*. The nibs contains 54% cocoa butter.

- The nibs are crushed into a thick liquor of cacao. It is then mixed with sugar and vanilla to make sweet chocolate.

- If the manufacturer adds milk solids, it becomes milk chocolate. This mixing which goes on for 72 hours is called *conching*.

- Cocoa butter, which was pressed from the seeds early on, is sometimes added to the chocolate to make it flow more easily and make it easier to dip or coat candies.

- When the cocoa butter has been pressed from the liquor of the cocoa, the portion that is left is in large hard cakes. This is crushed and sold as cocoa powder to make hot chocolate.

- Cocoa butter is used to make medicines, soap, and cosmetics.

- Making candy requires the chocolate to be heated, melted, and poured over what will be the base of the candy. Some candy is dipped.

- Chocolate products produced include baking chocolate, cocoa, milk chocolate, sweetened chocolate, and semisweet chocolate.

How Chocolate Is Made (cont.)

1. What is the taste of pure cacao?

   _____

2. What is the name of the case in which the beans come?

   _____

3. Why do they roast the cacao beans?

   _____

4. Where do they grow cacao beans?

   _____

5. What do you call the part of the cacao bean under the shell?

   _____

6. What is 54% of the cacao bean made of?

   _____

7. What is the synonym for stirring the chocolate?

   _____

8. What is the paste called that is made when you crush the nibs?

   _____

9. When the cocoa butter is pressed out of the chocolate liquid, what is left?

   _____

10. Name three products of the cacao tree.

   _____   _____   _____

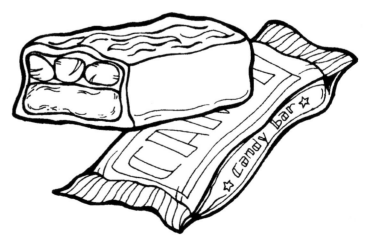

Chocolate-Lovers Survey

John loved chocolate a little too much. Do you like chocolate? How much chocolate do you think you eat? For one week, record each time you eat anything that contains chocolate or cocoa. List the items in the appropriate categories. Then, answer the questions at the bottom of the page.

Day	Breakfast	Lunch	Dinner	Snack
Sunday				
Monday				
Tuesday				
Wednesday				
Thursday				
Friday				
Saturday				
Subtotal				

Add all subtotals for a final total. Record the final total here: _____

1. If you eat chocolate at about the same rate all year, what do you think your average monthly chocolate consumption will be? _____

2. Based on the information above, what do you estimate your average yearly chocolate consumption to be? _____

Quiz Time!

Answer the following questions about chapters 10, 11, and 12 in sentences. You may use your book to find the answers.

1. What is in the place where the candy store had been?

   _____

2. What does Dr. Cranium think would cure John's problem?

   _____

3. What name does Dr. Cranium give to John's problem?

   _____

4. What happens when John kisses his mother's cheek?

   _____

   _____

5. What is in the windows of the candy shop when John returns to the shop?

   _____

   _____

   _____

   _____

6. Whom does John blame for his problems? _____

7. What kind of person could have a coin like the one John has?

   _____

   _____

   _____

8. What does the storekeeper say John has become? _____

9. What is the big choice that John has to make?

   _____

   _____

   _____

10. What finally happens to John's mother?

   _____

   _____

Homemade Elixir

Dr. Cranium gives John Midas a spoonful of Dr. Cranium's Elixir to "Clear the stomach and you clear the mind."

An elixir is a preparation formerly believed capable of keeping someone alive indefinitely and curing all that was wrong with them.

Dr. Cranium filled the spoon with an oily greenish-yellowish medicine that had yellowish-reddish lights glinting in it.

This is a label from a bottle of elixir. Create a label for a homemade elixir by completing the following:

- Name your special elixir on the top line.
- Tell what it does under the name.
- List at least five ingredients found in your elixir. (Be sure all the ingredients are safe to drink.)

_____ Elixir

Good for _____

_____and_____

Ingredients

_____   _____

_____   _____

_____   _____

_____   _____

Create a Story

The Chocolate Touch is an interesting tale of a boy who learns an important lesson. It is sometimes necessary to have difficulties before a person can learn a lesson. With two other people, create a story with three characters. Give one of the characters a problem to solve that allows him or her to learn a lesson in life. Before you create your story, discuss with your partners the details of the story. An outline is given below.

Title of the Story: _____

The Difficulty the Main Character Has to Face:

_____

_____

_____

_____

_____

_____

The Lesson That the Main Character Learns:

_____

_____

_____

_____

_____

_____

_____

Write your story on a separate sheet of paper. When you are finished, have one of the partners illustrate one scene in the story that can be used as a coloring page by the class. Have the title of the story written beneath the picture. Ask your teacher to copy your coloring page for the class. Read your finished story to the class.

Mapping Your School

John Midas couldn't find the candy store when he went with his father to look for it. Having a map can often help you find your way around an area. Maps can tell us where special things are by using a drawing.

For this activity you will create a picture map of your school. Begin by taking a tour of your school to identify where everything is located. A small sketch might help you remember where all the rooms are positioned. You will need a large piece of construction paper or butcher paper.

Cut out the picture boxes below and on page 35 and place them on the paper to show where everything is located at your school. When you have decided on the correct positions of all the pieces, glue them in place. If a room or facility at your school is not found in the pictures provided, create one and place it on the map.

If your school has two floors, you will need to make a separate map for each floor. Remember to leave room for the hallways. If there is anything unique about your school, such as a flower garden, a portable classroom, or a tennis court, be sure to allow for its placement before you glue the map pieces down.

Mapping Your School *(cont.)*

Survey of People's Needs

In *The Chocolate Touch* John felt that he needed only one thing, and Mrs. Midas felt that he needed another. Often people have different opinions about what they need or want.

Listed below are several people and some of their wishes. Not all are needs. Choose which are needs and which are wants. Discuss with the class why you think this is true.

Name	Wish	Need	Want
1. disabled boy	wheelchair		
2. mother of five children	babysitter		
3. 16-year-old boy	new car		
4. 10-year-old sister	TV in her room		
5. Uncle George	$1,000		
6. restaurant owner	new stove		
7. baseball player	a winning game		
8. 4th grader	vacation		
9. 10th grader	go to a dance		
10. a father	$100 of groceries		

Finding out what people you know want or need can be interesting.

Survey

- Survey 10 people you know and find out what they feel that they need or want more of. It is good to find out why they chose what they did, so don't forget to ask them why.

- Make a list on a chart like the one above on another piece of paper. Include the person's name, age, and wish. Check off whether it is a real need or just a want.

- Make sure you interview people from different age groups.

Chocolate Word Puzzles

There are many new words a reader learns when he or she reads a new book. Complete the puzzles below and on page 38 to see how much you remember about *The Chocolate Touch*.

Chocolate Puzzle One

Across

1. the sign on the lot when John went to find the candy store with his father
6. what has turned to chocolate during a test
7. the covering of the box of chocolates that John bought
10. what John was dunking for at Susan's party
12. the first thing that turned to chocolate for John
13. the person who tried to eat John's glove
14. what the letters are called on the coin John found
15. the person who read to John
18. the shape of Susan's coin after John bit it
21. the girl whom John liked
23. what the storekeeper said John was

Down

2. the person who sold John the box of chocolates that started his problem
3. how many candies were in the box John bought
4. John's homeroom teacher
5. Susan's last name
8. the boy who loved chocolate
9. the source of John's problem
11. a special medicine
16. a type of sticky candy
17. the name of John Midas' doctor
19. the instrument that John played that turned to chocolate
20. what a marrons glacés is
22. John's sister

Chocolate Word Puzzles (cont.)

Chocolate Puzzle Two is a word find. Listed below are 28 words from *The Chocolate Touch*. See if you can find them in the puzzle and circle them. Have a partner work with you. You can have a time limit or work at your own pace.

Chocolate Puzzle Two

S	S	E	N	H	S	I	F	L	E	S	G	E	A	T
U	U	E	G	S	L	A	I	T	I	N	I	G	Y	A
S	O	U	L	L	A	A	G	N	I	M	A	E	L	G
P	I	D	E	C	A	L	V	Z	R	M	G	F	T	U
I	C	E	E	L	A	C	I	T	C	A	R	P	F	O
C	A	Y	G	R	S	T	D	E	T	L	I	T	I	N
I	P	N	C	R	E	S	C	E	N	T	Y	M	W	G
O	S	E	N	P	G	T	C	E	H	S	S	U	S	R
U	R	T	P	D	F	M	S	K	P	C	A	I	Z	U
S	M	A	R	V	E	L	O	U	S	S	T	N	L	B
L	R	C	B	O	O	L	R	R	L	H	N	A	Q	B
Y	H	I	O	S	L	T	I	K	S	F	A	R	N	I
O	K	L	Q	S	E	L	D	X	G	E	F	C	N	S
A	O	E	H	D	N	N	X	V	I	Z	L	K	R	H
S	Q	D	H	B	G	U	T	T	E	R	G	I	A	D

absent	flustered	morsel	spacious
appetizing	gleaming	nougat	spectacles
cranium	glee	practical	spurted
crescent	gutter	rubbish	stroll
delicate	initials	selfishness	suspiciously
elixir	lace	snatched	swiftly
fantasy	marvelous	solo	tilted

Book Report Ideas

There are many ways to report on a book once you have finished reading it. After you have finished reading *The Chocolate Touch*, choose one of these ideas to use for a report. You might use one of the ideas below or an idea you have thought of yourself.

❏ **Once-Upon-a-Time Comic Strip**

Cut out 13 pieces of white paper that are 3" x 4" (8 cm x 10 cm) in size. On each rectangle of paper draw a cartoon of the most important event in each of the chapters of the book. When you have finished drawing and coloring the picture, write the words that each character may have said in the picture. Only after the words are completed do you draw a balloon around the words spoken. When all pictures are done, tape the pages together and fold in an accordion style. Use your last sheet for the cover. Share with your classmates.

❏ **Picture Book Posters**

Divide the story into separate events. Have each person be responsible for one event. Using large sheets of butcher paper, approximately 36" x 24" (91 cm x 61 cm), draw scenes from the part of the story that you choose to illustrate. Paint or color them clearly. Invite another class to see your giant picture book. Each student tells the part of the story that his or her picture represents while holding it up for the visitors to see. Perhaps the posters can be mounted around the room.

❏ **Lights Out, Lights On!**

Tell the story of the book by using the overhead projector to tell about each chapter of the book. With a marker draw and color pictures on a plastic sheet. Tell your part of the story as you show the picture. The first page should have the title, author, illustrator, and publisher.

❏ **Radio Show**

Tape around a portion of the book with sound effects and play it for the class. Do several sections, using a variety of sound effects (gurgling water, munching—newspaper in a bag, tearing off paper on the chocolate box, etc.). Present your radio show to the class or the entire school.

❏ **Tip Your Hat!**

Make a paper bag hat and tape sayings from the book to it. Roll a brown grocery bag several folds up from the opening side so it fits your head. Cut strips of white paper and print quotes from the book on them. Hang them from the hat with colored string and tape. Have a hat show!

❏ **Order! Order!**

Write sentences telling events that happened in the story. Print or write clearly. Put the papers in a plastic bag and give it to another student. Have the student place the slips of paper in the proper order.

❏ **Home Decorations!**

On book report day have each student decorate his or her desk with at least 10 different items that are related to the book he or she has read. Have students tell about each item and how it is related to the book.

❏ **Be a Character**

Choose one of the characters from the story and write a narrative from his or her point of view. Cover the main topics of each chapter. Dress up like the character and present your narrative to the class.

Chocolate Time Line

Below is information for a time line of the history of chocolate. The information includes other historical facts as reference points. Enlarge the time line on page 41 and glue it near the bottom of a large piece of construction paper. Cut out the time line strips below and place them in the appropriate places on the time line. Glue the strips in place.

Extension: Research other facts about chocolate and add related information and dates to the time line.

1492	Columbus comes to America.
1500	A chocolate drink known to the Aztecs comes to Europe through Spanish explorers.
1600	The chocolate drink becomes fashionable in Europe.
1620	The Pilgrims land.
1765	Chocolates are first manufactured in the United States in Dorchester, MA.
1776	The American Revolution begins.
1857	Milton Hershey is born.
1861	The Civil War begins.
1876	Switzerland perfects the process of making milk chocolate.
1877	Alexander Graham Bell invents the telephone.
1894	The Hershey Chocolate Company is started.
1900	The Hershey Bar comes out. It costs 5 cents.
1903	The Hershey Chocolate Corporation is established.
1905	The Wright brothers fly the first plane at Kitty Hawk, NC.
1906	The town of Derry Church becomes the town of Hershey, PA.
1909	The Milton Hershey School for orphaned boys is established.
1969	Neil Armstrong lands on the moon.
1990	Computers come into common use.

Chocolate Time Line *(cont.)*

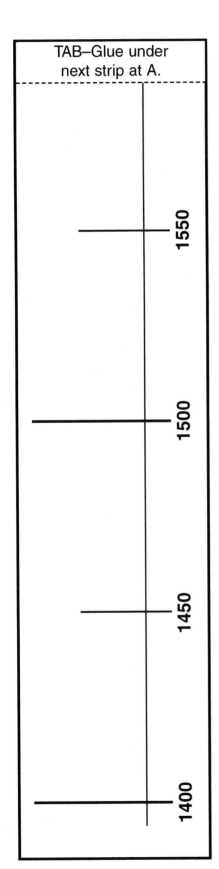

TAB–Glue under next strip at A.

1550

1500

1450

1400

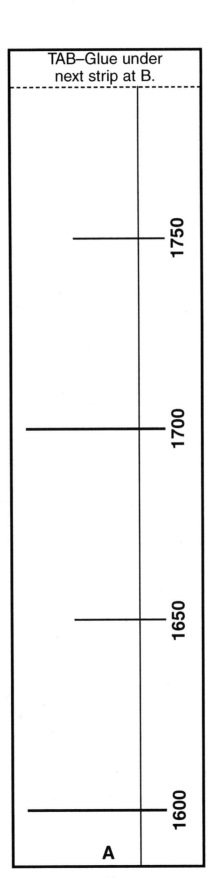

TAB–Glue under next strip at B.

1750

1700

1650

1600

A

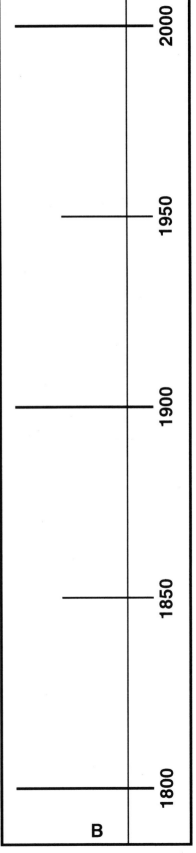

2000

1950

1900

1850

1800

B

Chocolate Party

Now that you have finished *The Chocolate Touch* and enjoyed the activities, it is a good time to share what you learned and to do some tasting. Here's what you need to do:

1. Send an invitation. It can be a simple note to the teacher of the class you would like to invite, or each student can make a special invitation. You can invite a lower grade to the party.

2. Make a banner or poster with the name of the book and author on it.

3. Use the recipe below to prepare a chocolate dip for the party.

Recipe for Chocolate Dip

Ingredients

- 16 ounces (450 g) of squares of semisweet chocolate, broken into small pieces
- 3 cups (750 mL) of condensed milk
- ⅔ cups (170 mL) of milk

Equipment

- paper plates, napkins
- fondue sticks or forks to dip with
- Crockpot or warmer that can melt chocolate

Directions

Melt the chocolate over low heat, stirring constantly. Pour in both milks and stir. Keep on warmer for the party or in a Crockpot. Use fondue sticks to spear desired food to dip. Swirl in chocolate, place on a plate, and eat. Suggested foods to dip: marshmallows, apple pieces, fresh strawberries, fresh peach sections, celery, chips, pretzels, bread, chunks of angel food cake, pineapple, cherries with stems, and bananas. You could also have chocolate milk to drink.

Things to do at the party:

1. Sing your rap and dance to it.

2. Read poems about chocolate.

3. Act out parts of the book.

4. Have a display on how chocolate is made. Explain the display to the guests.

Unit Test

Matching: Match the names of the characters with their best descriptions.

1. _____ John   a. a girl whom John liked

2. _____ storekeeper   b. the classroom teacher

3. _____ Mr. Midas   c. the music teacher

4. _____ Miss Plimsole   d. the person who discovered chocolitis

5. _____ Dr. Cranium   e. John's mother

6. _____ Mrs. Quaver   f. John's father

7. _____ Susan   g. a boy who ate too much chocolate

8. _____ Mrs. Midas   h. a pushy boy

9. _____ Mary   i. wanted John to change

10. _____ Spider Wilson   j. John's sister

True or False: Write true or false next to each statement below.

1. _____ John was a good boy who had one terrible fault.

2. _____ The storekeeper wanted John to buy more candy.

3. _____ John's father was kind.

4. _____ John learned his lesson.

5. _____ Susan Buttercup did not like John.

Sequence: Number these events in the order they occurred in the story.

_____ Everything John eats turns to chocolate.

_____ John always wanted chocolate.

_____ The storekeeper and John meet.

_____ The chocolate touch is taken away, and everything becomes normal.

_____ John finds a special coin.

Essay: Respond to the following on a separate sheet of paper.

Discuss the lesson that John learned from his experience with the chocolate touch. Explain what you have learned from reading and discussing this story.

Response

Explain the meaning of each of these quotations from *The Chocolate Touch*.

Chapter 1:   *Most of the time John was a very nice boy.*

Chapter 2:   *On one side there was a picture of a fat boy; on the other side were the letters J. M.—which was funny, John thought, because those letters happened to be his initials.*

Chapter 2:   *(Storekeeper) "In fact, it's the only kind of money I accept."*

Chapter 4:   *(Spider Wilson) "John's gone crazy! John's gone crazy!"*

Chapter 4:   *Susan could hardly believe her eyes. She had given John a complete circle of silver. He sadly handed back a crescent.*

Chapter 5:   *(Miss Plimsole) "This morning, children, we are going to have an important test."*

Chapter 6:   *"If you don't believe me," John retorted, "just you give me that skipping rope and I'll prove it."*

Chapter 7:   *Enviously John noticed a boy at a nearby table suck at straws dipped in a milk bottle that was dull with frost.*

Chapter 7:   *Until today John had always thought it was pretty dull to eat "sensible things" when there were sweeter food and drink to be had.*

Chapter 8:   *It sounded as though John were trying to play a soap-filled bubble pipe.*

Chapter 9:   *. . . indignant and angry at the world that had suddenly turned against him.*

Chapter 9:   *Then a terrible thing happened. The clear water in the bucket turned into dark-brown, sweet, liquid chocolate.*

Chapter 10:   *(Dr. Cranium) "I shall call it Cranium's Disease."*

Chapter 11:   *He kissed her wet cheek. His eyes were shut as his lips softly touched her, so he didn't see the change right away.*

Chapter 11:   *"Now, John," the storekeeper interrupted, "I must insist on honesty."*

Chapter 12:   *(Mrs. Midas) "You've had a very disturbing day, dear."*

Conversations

Work in size-appropriate groups to write and perform the conversations that might have occurred in each of the following situations. Write out your conversations on the back of this sheet so you and your partner will remember what to say. Act it out for the class.

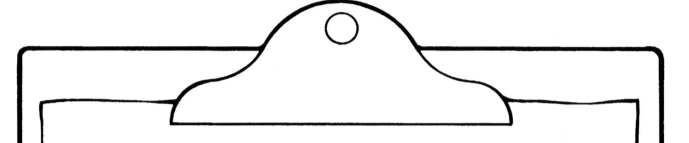

1. John has a conversation with his parents and tries to convince them that eating a lot of candy isn't bad for him. (three people)

2. The storekeeper and John discuss how John's mother can return to normal after being changed to chocolate. (two people)

3. John tries to convince his father that he really went to the candy store and received a magic chocolate candy. (two people)

4. John tries to convince Susan Buttercup and her friends that he can change things to chocolate. (three or more people)

5. Spider Wilson catches John eating a glove and wants to take it from John. (two people)

6. Susan and John dunk for apples, and the water turns to chocolate. (two people)

7. Mrs. Quaver, the music teacher, tells John how to play his trumpet part in the band, and John's trumpet turns to chocolate when he plays it. (two people)

8. Dr. Cranium discovers that John has chocolitis when he gives him the elixir. (two people)

9. John finds that his mother is upset and gives her a kiss that turns her to chocolate. (two people)

10. John chooses his lunch in the lunchroom and finds that everything he eats turns to chocolate. (one person)

Bibliography of Related Reading

Chocolate

Adoff, Arnold and Turi MacCombie. *Chocolate Dreams.* Lothrop, Lee and Shepard Books, 1989.

Ammon, Richard. *The Kid's Book of Chocolate.* Atheneum, 1987.

Cohen, Elizabeth Wolf and Valerie Barrett. *Chocolate Heaven.* J. G. Press, 1995.

Dineen, Jacqueline and John Yates. *Chocolate.* Carolrhoda Books, 1991.

Gaspero: Hershey Food Company. *Hershey's 1934 Cookbook-Revised.* Smithmark, 1993.

Jaspersohn, William. *Famous Amos Chocolate Chip Cookie Corporation.* Macmillan Pub., 1993.

Kindley, Jeffrey and Ellen Joy Sasaki. *Choco Louie.* Bantam Books, 1996.

Mitgutsch, Ali. *From Cacao Bean to Chocolate.* Carolrhoda Books, 1981.

O'Neill, Catherine and James W. Parker. *Let's Visit a Chocolate Factory.* Troll Associates, 1988.

Fantasy

Ahlberg, Janet and Allan. *The Clothes Horse and Other Stories.* Puffin, 1992.

Aiken, Joan. *Arabel's Raven.* Doubleday, 1975.

Atwater, Richard. *Mr. Popper's Penguins.* Little, 1992.

AVI (pen name of Avi Wortis). *Emily Upham's Revenge, or, How Deadwood Dick Saved the Banker's Niece: A Massachusetts Adventure.* Morrow, 1992.

Brink, Carol Ryrie. *Andy Buchram's Tin Men.* Viking, 1966.

Brown, Jeff. *Flat Stanley.* Harper, 1989.

Catling, Patrick Skene. *John Midas in the Dreamtime.* Morrow, 1987.

Charles, Prince of Whales. *The Old Man of Lochnagar.* Farrar, 1980.

Dahl, Roald. *Matilda.* Puffin, 1990.

Day, Alexandra and Christina Darling. *Mirror.* Farrar, Straus, and Giroux, 1997.

Disney, Walt. *Alice in Wonderland.* Gallery Books, 1991.

Elish, Dan. *The Worldwide Dessert Contest.* Bantam, 1990.

Feinberg, Anna. *Wiggy and Boa.* Houghton, 1990.

Gifaldi, David. *Gregory, Maw and the Mean One.* Houghton, 1992.

Kaner, Etta. *I Am Not Jenny.* Groundwood Books, 1991.

Lofting, Hugh. *The Story of Doctor Dolittle.* Delacorte, 1998.

Ridley, Philip. *Krindlekrax: Or, How Ruskin Splinter Battled a Horrible Monster and Saved His Entire Neighborhood.* Knopf, 1992.

York, Carol Beach. *Pudmuddles.* Harper, 1993.

Sound Recording

The Chocolate Touch. Cassettes. Listening Library, 1992. 1 hr. 18 min.

Answer Key

Page 12

1. It is more interesting. One could answer that it tells more about what John was like.
2. John loves boiled candy, cotton candy, licorice all sorts, old-fashioned toffee, candied orange and lemon slices, crackerjacks, jellybeans, fudge, black-currant lozenges, nougat, marrons glacés, acid drops, peppermint sticks, lollipops, marshmallows, and, most of all, chocolates.
3. He knows he has the chocolate touch.
4. John's doctor is named Cranium. Dr. Cranium uses his head to help with illnesses.
5. Yes. You could say they try to understand why John is upset. His father goes with him to find the candy shop. John's parents take him to the doctor when he isn't feeling well.
6. He doesn't want his parents to know that he has so much candy.
7. It has his initials on it.
8. The toothpaste changes to chocolate.
9. One chocolate is in the box.
10. Yes or no. The student will explain.

Page 15

1. sugar
2. milk
3. cocoa butter
4. chocolate
5. soya lecithin
6. vanillin
7. almonds

Page 18

1. All that John puts into his mouth turns to chocolate.
2. John is eating his glove.
3. John bites into Susan's birthday coin.
4. Everything that his lips touch turns to chocolate.
5. John really wants water.
6. John is beginning to not want the chocolate touch.
7. They might say that he is imagining his magic.
8. His gloves turn to chocolate. The part of Susan's coin that John bites turns to chocolate. Water turns to chocolate. His pencil turns to chocolate.
9. The students could say: Don't tell people about his magic. Don't touch other people's things. Don't bite anything that is not food. Don't let his lips touch anyone.
10. Students could say that too much of anything is not good.

Page 21

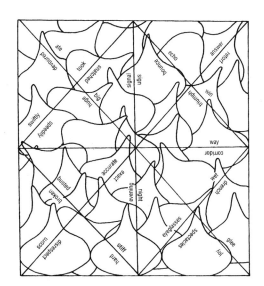

Page 24

1. The boy is eating real food.
2. His major fear is how he would feed himself.
3. John tries dropping the food directly down his throat.
4. More than the food is turning to chocolate.
5. He plays the trumpet. It changes to chocolate.
6. He wants someone to blame for his problems.
7. When his mother said he'd get a reward of a piece of chocolate after supper for coming home early, John replies, "I hate it!" Also, he said he isn't going to Susan's party.
8. She makes him the captain of the boys' team in the dunking game. Also, Susan smiles at John and says, "I'm glad you came."
9. The last game is ducking for apples.
10. A student might answer that having all his food turn to chocolate is bad, but now it is worse because other things are changing, too.

Answer Key *(cont.)*

Page 29

1. Bitter
2. Pods
3. To burst their shells
4. Tropical countries, Mexico, Central America, South America, and Africa
5. Nibs
6. Cocoa butter
7. Conching
8. Cocoa liquor
9. Cocoa powder
10. Accept any three of the following: cocoa, milk chocolate, baking chocolate, semisweet chocolate.

Page 31

1. In its place is a lot with a "For Sale" sign.
2. Dr. Cranium's Elixir would cure it.
3. Cranium's Disease or Chocolitis is the name he gives it.
4. She turns to chocolate.
5. In the windows are a chocolate trumpet, a chocolate pencil, a silver dollar with a piece bitten out of it, a cafeteria tray littered with chocolate utensils, and the remains of a chocolate lunch.
6. John blames the storekeeper.
7. Someone who is greedy could have such a coin.
8. He says John has become greedy.
9. John has to choose to keep the chocolate touch or to have his mother back.
10. She is returned to normal.

Page 37

Across

1. FORSALE
6. PENCIL
7. CELLOPHANE
10. APPLES
12. TOOTHPASTE
13. SPIDERWILSON
14. INITIALS
15. FATHER
18. CRESCENT
21. SUSAN
23. GREEDY

Down

2. STOREKEEPER
3. ONE
4. PLIMSOLE
5. BUTTERCUP
8. JOHNMIDAS
9. CHOCOLATE
11. ELIXIR
16. TOFFEE
17. CRANIUM
19. TRUMPET
20. CANDY
22. MARY

Page 38

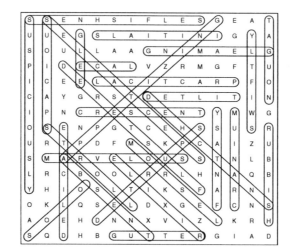

Page 43

Matching:

1. g	6. c
2. i	7. a
3. f	8. e
4. b	9. j
5. d	10. h

True or False:

1. True
2. False
3. True
4. True
5. False

Sequence: 4, 1, 3, 5, 2

Page 44

Accept all reasonable responses.

Page 45

Perform the conversations in the classroom. Ask whether the conversations are realistic and match the characters. Have a class discussion.